Mindfulness
for Kids Who
Worry

**Calming Exercises
to Overcome
Anxiety**

Mindfulness *for Kids Who* Worry

**Calming Exercises
to Overcome
Anxiety**

KATIE AUSTIN,
LCSW-C

ROCKRIDGE
PRESS

Interior and Cover Designer: Julie Schrader
Art Producer: Sara Feinstein
Editor: Eliza Kirby
Production Editor: Ashley Polikoff
Illustrations © Sam Kalda.
Author photo courtesy of © Bella Baby Photography, Margarita Stamatelopoulos.

ISBN: 978-1-64152-766-8
RO

To Ellie Gray, my little Zen master
and profound thinker.

Contents

A Letter to Kids

Hi, friend, and welcome to your mindfulness journey! Together we will learn how to manage our worries with mindfulness.

Sometimes we need worries. They can tell us that something is wrong, remind us to be careful, or help us plan things out. But worrying too much is not helpful. It can be tiring and uncomfortable. It can stop us from doing things that we love to do. Sometimes it can even make us sick.

If you feel like you worry too much, you can change that. This book will be your guide in learning how to manage these worries even when it seems impossible. It will teach you about mindfulness—our ability to find peace, even with our most uncomfortable feelings. We will always have uncomfortable feelings, but that doesn't mean that they get to control our lives. With the skills you learn in this book, you can take back control and get back to doing the things you love to do.

So let's get started! You can either read the next page of the book with an adult or jump ahead to chapter one.

A Letter to Grown-Ups

Welcome, parents and guardians! This book is designed for children ages six to ten who struggle with worry and anxiety. While anxiety is a normal human response to uncomfortable situations, it can become a problem when it starts to disrupt our ability to participate in daily activities and do the things that we enjoy. If you feel your child struggles with anxiety, then this book is for them (and you)! In it, you will find stories and strategies to help them understand why they feel the way they do and how to manage their worries with mindfulness. It's important to note that this book is not a substitute for therapy but rather a companion for your child as they work to regain control of their worries.

Children in this age group may not be able to effectively verbalize how they are feeling. Some indicators that they are struggling with anxiety are an upset stomach, especially around specific situations; increased irritability; difficulty falling asleep or staying asleep; avoiding activities or people that they used to enjoy; seemingly inexplicable crying spells; changes in motivation; emotional meltdowns; or changes in appetite.

This book will help your child understand what's going on in their bodies and brains and will give them tools to manage their anxiety more effectively. You are an important part of your child's mindfulness journey. I encourage you to take an active role in this process.

Read along with them, talk to them about what they have learned, familiarize yourself with the concepts in this book, and offer the strategies discussed when they are struggling. With mindfulness, practice leads to success. The more they practice these skills, the more successful they will be in managing their anxiety.

CHAPTER ONE

Mindfulness: What's That About?

Mindfulness is the practice of being present in each moment. It means paying attention fully to what's going on in our bodies, inside our heads, and around us in our environment. Sounds pretty simple, right? It is! When we hear the birds singing outside or smell something cooking in the oven, it catches our attention. We notice it. We enjoy it and we stay present with it, feeling the good feelings that come from what our senses are telling us.

But mindfulness can sometimes be hard when we notice something that we do not enjoy. When we feel a big, overwhelming feeling, we don't want it to stay; we want it to go away! Or when we have a scary thought, we do our best to think about something else. When we are uncomfortable, it can be hard to "sit with" those scary feelings or thoughts. This is totally normal, because we don't want to feel that way. We want to feel better!

But here's the thing: When we try to avoid things that make us uncomfortable, it can make it even more difficult to feel better. This is where mindfulness comes in. It's a set of skills to help us get through the uncomfortable stuff. It's not going to take those big feelings away, but it will help us access a strength that sometimes we forget we have. It's the strength to get through something difficult, and you have it in your mind right now!

How Can Mindfulness Help with My Worries?

Sometimes we feel worried because we think too much about the future. We are supposed to think about the future sometimes; it's how we stay safe and take care of ourselves and others. For example, we think about what we want to eat for lunch so that we won't be too hungry at soccer practice after school. We get directions to a new place so that we won't get lost. These are all helpful thoughts that prepare us for the future.

But sometimes our brains can trick us. We might think about the future too much, making it hard to focus on what's right in front of us. For example, if you spend all weekend worrying about a big test next week, it could be hard to focus on studying. These worries are not helpful, and can keep you from doing your best to prepare. Plus, if you spend too much time worrying, you could miss out on fun things to do that weekend, like hanging out with friends or playing outside.

By slowing down and being mindful, we are able to notice and listen to our helpful thoughts, and let the unhelpful worries pass us by. When we practice mindfulness, we can learn to stop believing our brains when they're trying to trick us. This helps us worry less, do our best, and have more fun.

Let's Get To It! Skills for Being Mindful

Let's talk about what mindfulness means for our brains, breath, and bodies, and how we experience what's going on around us. All of these areas are connected. This means that practicing mindfulness skills for our breath can help calm down our bodies, and practicing mindfulness skills for our bodies can help calm down our brains. This means that practicing just one skill in one of these areas can help our whole selves feel better.

For each area, we will talk about different skills you can use to slow down and be more mindful. This might take some practice, but once you get better at it, you'll be able to use these skills to pause and notice what's going on—giving yourself the chance to better manage your worries.

YOUR BRAIN

Slowing down and trying to be aware of what we are thinking is a way to be mindful. When thoughts pop into your head, it is normal to follow them on to the next thought. For example, if you are talking to your parent about plans for the weekend, they might mention that a friend is coming over tomorrow. Then you start to think about the fun things you want to do with your friend. It is easy to get caught up in a trail of thoughts. But before you know it, your parent is done talking and you've missed the rest of the plan for the weekend because you were thinking about other things. Instead of listening and staying present in the conversation, your brain was busy thinking.

Let's try something! I want you to stop thinking. Close your eyes, and stop your thoughts. Don't think about anything. You can't, right? Because it's not possible. Our brains are always thinking.

Instead of trying to stop or control our thoughts, let's try just noticing them. Close your eyes, and notice what you are thinking. Picture your thoughts as bubbles floating by. Sometimes there are a lot, sometimes only a few. Sometimes they stay for a while, while others are quick to pop and go away. Notice each one, but let it pass you by. Our thoughts, like the bubbles, are temporary, and before we know it, they are gone.

YOUR BREATH

Just as we are always thinking, we are also always breathing. Sometimes our breath comes faster, like when we exercise or when we are nervous. Sometimes it is slower, like when we are reading a book or falling asleep.

Noticing your breath is another way to practice mindfulness. Practice for a moment. Put a hand on your belly, and notice how your belly rises and falls with each breath. Once you notice your breath, it can start to change. That's okay. Do your best to just observe it. Is your breath fast right now? Or is it slow? Notice how with each inhale you are filled with energy, and with each exhale your body relaxes.

Checking in with your breath keeps you connected to your body. It is a reminder that you are here and you are safe. Your breath got you here, to this moment. And it will get you through the next one.

YOUR BODY

Your body is constantly working. Most of the time, we don't even realize everything that our bodies do because we are so busy doing other things. But when we slow down to notice what our bodies are feeling, we realize that we are full of sensation.

Get into a comfortable position. You can either sit or lie down. If possible, keep your back straight so your breath can come easily. Close your eyes (or find something still to look at). Starting at your head and moving down all the way to your feet, take a moment to check in with how the different parts of your body feel. How does your head feel? Your shoulders? Your arms? Your back? Your belly? Your legs? And your feet?

Are there any areas that are tight or tense? As you checked in with each part of your body, how did it feel? Did you feel little sensations you hadn't noticed before? Like how your shirt feels against your back? Or the way your hair tickles your face?

Slowing down and doing a quick scan of your body helps you be more aware of what you are feeling. You realize that your body is full of sensations that you might not have noticed. We can tune in to our bodies and understand what is going on in our brains.

OUTSIDE

Now we are going to venture outside of ourselves and see how mindfulness can help us be more aware of what's going on around us. Our bodies have five senses that they use to take in information from the world around us: sight, sound, taste, smell, and touch. We are going to explore the information that these senses take in, examining each one as we go.

Get comfortable again. Now I want you to pay attention to what's going on around you and notice one thing from each of your senses.

Start with sight. Notice something interesting that you can see: a color, a shape, or a detail that maybe you hadn't noticed before.

Now sound. Notice something that you can hear. Is it close? Is it far? Do you enjoy the sound?

How about touch? What can you feel that is around you? It is rough or smooth? Soft or hard? Warm or cold?

And smell? What can you smell? Anything? Is it a strong smell? Or is faint?

How about taste? What can you taste right now? Are there any lingering tastes in your mouth from the last meal you ate? How about a sip of water? How does that taste?

By taking a moment to check in with each sense, we are noticing the environment around us and becoming more present in the world around us.

NOW, EVERYTHING TOGETHER!

You now have tools that you can practice anytime, anywhere to slow down and be more mindful. We are going to bring all these skills together for a mindful check-in. This is something you can do when you notice that you are starting to feel worried. It only takes a couple of minutes, and you can do it wherever you are.

- **CHECK IN WITH YOUR THOUGHTS:** Notice what you are thinking. Notice how your thoughts come and go.

- **CHECK IN WITH YOUR BREATHING:** Notice, don't change, your breath.

- **CHECK IN WITH YOUR BODY:** Notice each area of your body. How does it feel?

- **CHECK IN WITH YOUR SENSES:** What do you see, hear, taste, smell, and feel?

Practicing these check-ins will help you be more aware of what is going on when you are worried. By tuning in to your brain, body, breath, and environment, you are able to tune out your worries.

Through the exercises in this book, you'll use your mindfulness skills to manage your worries and help you feel less anxious. Let's get started!

CHAPTER TWO

Science Fair Project Panic

The science fair is here, and Ella is so excited! She has been working hard for weeks on her project about evaporation. She came to school today ready to set up her poster board at a table in the gym. But on her way to class, she found out from a friend that before they set up their presentations, they have to present their project to the whole class—*and* it will be part of their grade. How had Ella missed this? She had no idea! Ella knows this project inside and out, but she has never liked speaking in front of groups of people. She does not feel prepared.

When she gets to class, her teacher informs everyone that they will be presenting in alphabetical order. Now Ella is only two people away from presenting. She starts to feel her heart pounding in her chest and notices that her hands feel clammy. Uh oh, not again! She remembers the last time she was supposed to speak in front of her class. She was so nervous that she ran out of the classroom. By the time she made it back, she had missed her chance to present. Her teacher let her present alone later in the day, but she didn't get full credit.

Ella starts thinking about everything that could go wrong when it's her turn. Will everything that happened before happen again? She worked so hard on this project. What if she doesn't get full credit? What if people notice that she's anxious and think something is wrong with her? What if they make fun of her? What if she throws up in front of everyone?

Awareness

Being aware of what's going on in the present moment is an important first step to being more mindful. Our bodies will send us signals, or warning signs, when we start to feel uncomfortable—like when Ella noticed that her head was pounding and her hands felt clammy. Her body was telling her that she was starting to feel worried and anxious.

Once you notice your body starting to feel this way, it's important to check in with your thoughts. Our thoughts can be automatic—meaning they just happen—so we might not even be aware of them if we don't check in. These automatic thoughts are normal. They're another way for our brains to warn us that something is not right. But they aren't always helpful.

Ella's brain and body were sensing that something was about to happen that would be uncomfortable for her. She was remembering the bad things that had happened the last time she was in this situation, and imagining the things that could go wrong this time. These thoughts were coming fast. They seemed to be outside of her control. But while her brain was *trying to* help her, these thoughts weren't *doing a good job* of helping. Instead, they were making it harder for her to focus on her presentation and making her believe that she might not be able to do it.

It can be hard to check in with our thoughts without getting caught up in them. The secret is pausing, taking a step back, and just "watching" our thoughts. Let's try it!

Mindfulness Exercise

Make yourself comfortable, close your eyes (or if you don't want to, focus on one unmoving spot), and picture yourself sitting on top of a hill. Notice your thoughts as they pass by below you like cars and trucks on a highway. Some thoughts might stick around, like a slow, loud truck going around a corner, and some thoughts might come and go quickly, like a fast, red convertible. Either way, those thoughts are down there, at the bottom of the hill. And you are up at the top of the hill, just observing them. Notice them, and how they come and go.

Watch Your Thoughts

ACTIVITY: Find a comfortable place to sit, somewhere quiet where you won't be interrupted. Take five minutes to write down any thoughts that come to you. You can write phrases, sentences, or single words to describe what you're thinking. Try not to control your thoughts, but—like the exercise we just did—observe them as they come, and write them down. It's okay if you get caught up and distracted by them. Take a deep breath, notice that you are distracted, and gently bring yourself back to the activity.

Write here:

ACTIVITY: Now that you've written down your thoughts, put a circle around the comfortable thoughts. These could be simple observations about how you are feeling or things happening around you. Or they could be more enjoyable thoughts about things you are looking forward to or people you love. Next, put a square around the thoughts that were uncomfortable for you—the thoughts that you wished would go away when they popped into your head.

Sometimes, uncomfortable thoughts can be helpful because they tell us something important, like something we need to prepare for or change. For example, if we have a presentation next week, we might not like thinking about it, but it reminds us to prepare and do our best. And sometimes uncomfortable thoughts aren't helpful, like with Ella. She was so worried about all the bad stuff that could happen that it made it harder for her to get ready for her presentation.

Being aware of our thoughts is important because our thoughts impact how we feel. Our thoughts come and they go. These simple steps—pausing, taking a step back, and "watching" our thoughts—can help us worry less and feel better!

Wrap Up

While Ella waits for her turn to present, she can practice the mindfulness exercise on page 17. By picturing herself on a hill away from her thoughts, Ella is becoming more aware of her thoughts, without getting caught up in them. This will help her calm down and feel less anxious. And when her teacher calls her name, she will be ready to give her presentation!

CHAPTER THREE

Alone in the Dark

Sophia loves bedtime. She gets to pick out her favorite pajamas, brush her teeth with her princess toothbrush, and snuggle up under the covers with her favorite stuffed animals. She even gets to cuddle and read stories with Grandma! But once Grandma leaves and turns off the light, Sophia starts to worry.

She has many thoughts. She wonders if her fish is hungry—she can't remember if she fed him. She thinks about her dog and hopes that Grandma remembers to bring him inside. What if her dog stays outside all night? He will be cold and sad. Then she starts to think about her day tomorrow. She remembers that she needs to wear her sneakers for gym class so she can play capture the flag. But she can't remember where she put them. Did she leave them upstairs or downstairs? Are they in the car? Sophia is getting more and more worried. What if she can't find them? She won't be able to play the game!

Her thoughts start coming faster and getting more uncomfortable. She suddenly feels cold all over, and her mouth is dry. She is having a hard time falling asleep. She feels jumpy. Sophia hears a thump from downstairs and thinks that a burglar must be in the house. Now Sophia is really scared, and she's convinced that something bad is going to happen.

Your Thoughts Aren't a Crystal Ball

Here's a secret: We can't predict the future! But you already knew that, didn't you? It's our brains' job to try to figure out what *might* happen in the future so that we can be prepared. But there is no way to know for sure. So our brains do their best with the information they have.

When we are worried or anxious, it can be hard for our brains to figure out what is possible (meaning what *could* happen) and what is probable (meaning what will *most likely* happen). Our brains think that everything is probable, even if it's just possible. That is not realistic, and it can cause problems for us. Think about Sophia: Her brain heard a noise and is telling her that something bad is going to happen. This is a problem. She should be sleeping, not worrying!

Mindfulness can help us figure out if our thoughts are accurate or if our brains are tricking us. When we feel strong emotions, it can be hard to know if what we are thinking is *possible* or *probable*. Sophia is already pretty worried when she hears a noise downstairs. Because she is worried, it is hard to figure out if her thoughts are accurate. So she thinks about the bad things that *could* happen—like a burglar being in the house—and her brain convinces her that they *will* happen. This makes her even more scared!

When we practice mindfulness, we slow down and look at our thoughts. This allows us to decide for ourselves if what we are thinking is possible or probable. Let's try it!

Mindfulness Exercise

Get into a comfortable position. You can either sit or lie down. If possible, keep your back straight so you can breathe easily. Close your eyes (or find something still to look at). Take a couple of moments to focus on your breathing. Breathe in. Breathe out.

Now imagine that you are sitting in a garden full of beautiful flowers. There are flowers of all shapes and sizes and many different colors. You notice that there are also some weeds in your garden. They are taking up space and not letting the beautiful flowers grow.

Now imagine your thoughts are these flowers and weeds. It's your job to figure out which thoughts are the flowers (reliable and helpful thoughts) and which thoughts are the weeds (unreasonable and unhelpful thoughts).

As you gently examine each thought you have, ask yourself these two questions:

- Is this thought true?

- Is this thought helpful for me?

If you answered "no" to either of these questions, then the thought is a weed. Gently pull it out of your garden. That thought is not helpful for you, and you need room for your helpful thoughts to grow.

It Didn't Happen!

ACTIVITY: **How do we figure out if something we are worried about is possible or probable? We follow the evidence!**

When you are worried about something that could happen, pause and take a moment and try to prove that your worry isn't true. Make a list of the other possibilities. Let's use Sophia's story as an example. She hears a loud noise and is worried that a burglar could be in the house. Are there any other possibilities? Maybe Grandpa came home from work? Maybe the dog jumped off the couch? Maybe a box fell off the pantry shelf? If there are other possibilities for the cause of our worries, then our worry is possible, not probable.

ACTIVITY: Think about three times you were worried about something that didn't happen. In the left column, write down what you thought would happen. Across from each worry, in the right column, write down what actually happened. The next time you are worried about something that could happen in the future, remind yourself of these three times. Remind yourself that your thoughts aren't a crystal ball!

WORRIES	WHAT ACTUALLY HAPPENED

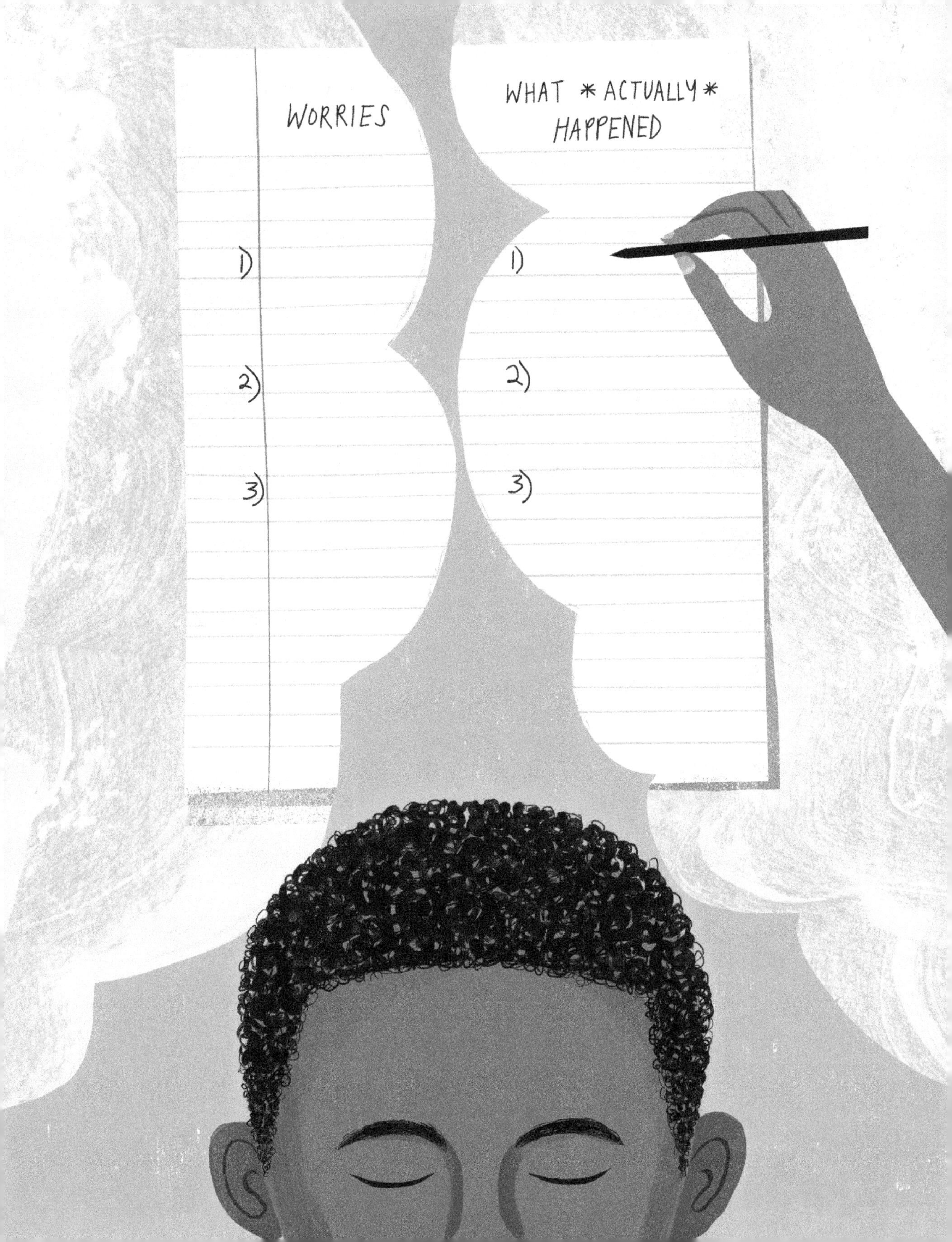
WORRIES
1)
2)
3)
WHAT *ACTUALLY* HAPPENED
1)
2)
3)

Wrap Up

While Sophia is lying in bed, she can practice the mindfulness exercise on page 25 and practice "weeding out" the uncomfortable thoughts that aren't helping her fall asleep. As she "weeds out" the unhelpful thoughts that are making her anxious, she will find herself more calm and able to sleep.

CHAPTER FOUR

Late for School, Again!

At breakfast, Noah's younger sister spills oatmeal all over her shirt. Dad tries to clean it up, but she insists that she needs a whole new outfit. Dad takes her upstairs to change, leaving Noah alone at the breakfast table. Noah looks at his watch. It's 8:20. He knows they have to leave by 8:30 to get to school by 9:00. Noah can hear his sister crying upstairs, refusing each new outfit Dad offers. He is worried that they won't be able to get out the door on time. Then he notices the unpacked lunch bags on the counter and realizes that Dad hasn't even packed their lunches yet! Now he is sure they are going to be late.

He wonders if he should pack his own lunch, but he doesn't even know which container to put his sandwich in. Maybe he should call Mom at work. But she's probably already in a meeting, and he knows he's only supposed to call for emergencies. Is this an emergency? Noah's head starts to fill up with thoughts, making it hard to decide what to do. He starts to feel hopeless. No matter what he does, he is going to be late for school. He's so busy with his worries, he forgets to eat his breakfast or feed the dog like Dad asked.

The more Noah thinks about it, the more anxious and hopeless he feels. He remembers feeling embarrassed when he walked into class late last week. He worries about what the teacher will say to him. He wonders if anyone will notice him coming in after the bell. He knows that if he is late three times this quarter, he will get a lunch detention. How many times has he been late so far? He can't remember. Noah thinks about how much he loves lunch. He can't miss lunch! It's the only chance to talk to his friends all day. Noah's day is ruined!

His thoughts start to come faster and faster. Now his stomach hurts.

Rewrite Your Thoughts

We learned in the last chapter that our thoughts are not always reliable. We can choose which thoughts to believe. Well, we have another cool power that we can use: We have the power to change our thoughts! We can rewrite them into thoughts that are more helpful and comfortable.

How do we do this? We find a different perspective, or a different way to think about things. Our thoughts are powerful, and when we have uncomfortable thoughts, they can make us feel worried, anxious, scared, sad, or mad. The same is true for when we have comfortable and enjoyable thoughts. They can help us feel happier and more hopeful, confident, and calm, and those feelings can help us manage our worries better.

Let's look at Noah's story. The more he thought about being late, the more worried and hopeless he felt. The more worried and hopeless he felt, the harder it was for him to take action. Spending time worrying takes away from the time that we have to fix the problem. Sometimes it can even cause us to do things that make the problem worse. Remember, Noah was so worried about being late that he forgot to eat his breakfast and feed his dog!

When he sees the unpacked lunches, Noah thinks that he is "for sure" going to be late. This makes him feel pretty hopeless—that there was nothing he could do to change things. What would have happened if Noah had been able to rewrite his thoughts? Let's try it!

Mindfulness Exercise

Get into a comfortable position. You can either sit or lie down. If possible, keep your back straight so you can breathe easily. Close your eyes (or find something still to look at). Take a few moments to connect to your breath. Breathe in. Breathe out.

Now, I want you to let your thoughts come. Some of them will be comfortable, and some of them will be uncomfortable. Let them all in. When you notice one that is uncomfortable, imagine yourself holding a giant pencil. Erase that uncomfortable thought, and write a new one. Write your thought in a way that is true, but less uncomfortable for you. For example, if you think to yourself, "I can't do this," erase that thought and write, "This will be hard, and I will try my best." If a thought comes along that is too difficult to rewrite, let that thought go, and gently continue with the exercise.

When you are ready, open your eyes.

Rewriting for You

ACTIVITY: Write down something you are wo[rried about in] much detail as you can. Underneath it, rewrite y[our thought. Try] to write your thought so that it is still true but no lo[nger scary,] like in the mindfulness exercise. Whenever you are feel[ing] worried, turn to this page for a reminder that you can alway[s] rewrite your thoughts.

_____

_____

_____

_____

Sometimes it can be hard to think about things differently if you are upset. Before you do this activity, practice the mindfulness exercise on page 35. Then, if you are still having a hard time rewriting your thought, try the next activity.

...is hard, it can be helpful ...a happy one. Take a ...g that makes you happy. It ...l, a drawing of your ...of anything that makes

How do you feel after drawing the picture? Are you happy? Calm? You can feel this feeling wherever you go, just by looking at this image or picturing it in your head. Turn to this page whenever you need a happy thought!

Wrap Up

While Noah is sitting at his kitchen table, waiting for his sister and dad to come back downstairs, he can practice the mindfulness exercise on page 37 and rewrite his uncomfortable thoughts. For example, when he thinks "We are definitely going to be late, and I can't do anything about it," he can change it to "There are some things that need to be done before we can leave." By rewriting this thought, Noah is giving himself the power to take action, which will make him feel less worried.

Because remember: What we think influences how we feel and what we do. Instead of feeling hopeless—like nothing he did would matter—he can do something to fix his problem, which can then help him feel less worried. He can pack the lunches, finish eating his breakfast, and feed the dog. This will help them stay closer to their schedule, and they may even get to school on time.

CHAPTER FIVE

Oh, No! Lost in the Supermarket

Isla is so excited! She gets to go to the supermarket with her favorite aunt. Her aunt even told her that she can pick out some ice cream for their sleepover tonight. When Isla gets to the supermarket, she wants to pick out the ice cream right away. But first they need to pick out food for dinner. They get close to the freezer section, and Isla is so excited that she hurries over to the ice cream, telling her aunt what she's doing as she walks away.

When she finally gets to the ice cream, Isla can't decide which one to pick. Chocolate or mint–chocolate chip? She loves both! Isla finally makes a choice and goes back to where she left her aunt. But her aunt is not there! Isla's heart starts to beat quickly. She thinks, "Oh, no! Where is she?" Isla looks down the rest of the aisle, but her aunt's not there. Isla goes to the next aisle, but she's not there either!

Isla's thoughts start to come faster and faster. She's alone. She doesn't know where her aunt is. She doesn't know anyone else here. Isla is panicking! Isla thinks, "How will I find my aunt? What if she left without me? Why didn't I listen to her and wait to get the ice cream together?" Isla is getting worried. The more worried she is, the harder it is for her to think straight. She wonders, "What should I do?" Isla tries to think of how she could find her aunt, but her worries keep getting in the way. Isla thinks, "What if she never comes back to get me? How will I get back home?" Isla's palms get sweaty, and she starts to feel dizzy. Isla needs to find a place to sit down.

Becoming Friends with Your Thoughts

Now that we understand a little bit more about how our brains work, it's important to accept our brains for all that they do. This means accepting even our uncomfortable thoughts. With these thoughts, our brains are just doing their job—they're trying to help us be prepared and stay safe. We will always have uncomfortable thoughts, but it can be hard to let these uncomfortable thoughts in. We don't want to have them, because they make us feel worried. We don't like feeling that way.

Sometimes we spend a lot of time trying to avoid or ignore our uncomfortable thoughts. But remember, our worries can tell us that something is wrong. If we don't listen to our worries, then we can end up feeling even more worried later. If we don't listen to them, then we can't fix what's wrong.

When we take the time to accept our thoughts just as they are, we no longer have to try to avoid them. We are able to befriend them, and they become less scary. We take back control of our worries by *choosing* to let them in. Once we accept our worries, we accept that there is a problem, and we can move forward and try to solve it.

Let's look at Isla's story. She was lost in the supermarket and feeling scared. Her thoughts and feelings were important. They were telling her that something was wrong and that she needed to find her aunt. But the more she thought about what was going on, the scarier it felt. The more afraid she felt, the harder it was for Isla to do anything. Eventually she was so upset that she had to sit down.

What do you think would have happened if Isla had taken a moment to pause and befriend her scary thoughts? Would that have made it easier for her to look for her aunt?

Let's try it!

Mindfulness Exercise

Get into a comfortable position. You can either sit or lie down. If possible, keep your back straight so you can breathe easily. Close your eyes (or find something still to look at). Take a couple of moments to focus on your breathing. Breathe in. Breathe out.

I want you to picture yourself in a simple, one-room house. What do you see in your house? Is there a cozy place to sit? Are there pretty pictures on the wall? Are there many colors, or just a few? It can be anything you want it to be.

Now, what do you smell in your house? Freshly baked cookies? Or is the window open, letting you smell the flowers outside?

What do you hear in your house? Are there birds outside your window? Is a radio on? Any noise that is comforting to you can be in your house.

What do you feel in your house? Are there any comfortable blankets? Is the floor hard and cool beneath your feet, or is it soft and comfy? What is the temperature in your house? Do you like it a little warmer or cooler? Is there a fan on? Is warm sunlight coming through a window?

Now what do you taste in your house? Have you eaten anything yummy or maybe taken a sip of something cool and refreshing?

Now that we are done creating your house, take a minute to enjoy how comfortable and safe it is.

Then, when you are ready, I want you to picture a door. You hear a gentle knock on the door. When you open the door, you find your worry standing there. You want to slam the door in your worry's face, but try this instead: Greet your worry and talk to it. When you're ready, invite your worry inside. The worry can't break anything in your house. Your house is your safe place, and your worry is just stopping by. Your worry will leave, and everything will be as it was.

When you're ready, say goodbye to your worry and close the door. Go back into your safe place. Check back in with everything you see, hear, taste, and feel in your house. Know that you are safe. When you are ready, open your eyes.

Talk to Your Thoughts

ACTIVITY: Draw a picture of yourself talking to your worry as a friend. Write down what you are saying to each other. What is your worry saying to you? What is your worry's message? What is your worry trying to help you understand? And how do you respond to your worry? Maybe you thank it. Or give it a high five. Or ask it to leave for a while.

Remember, our worries can be scary, but they are our brains' way of trying to tell us something.

Draw your picture here:

ACTIVITY: Draw a picture of one of your worries complimenting you. For example, if Isla is scared to go back to the supermarket after getting lost, she could draw a picture of a supermarket telling her, "Wow, you are so brave! You were scared last time you saw me, but you came back anyway! That's so cool!"

When we befriend and talk to our thoughts, we are able to understand them and use them to help us feel better.

Draw your picture here:

Wrap Up

When Isla first realizes that she has lost her aunt, she is worried!
She starts to panic, and her thoughts start to come fast. This makes
her even more worried. She has a hard time clearing her head and
coming up with a plan to find her aunt. While standing in the gro-
cery aisle, Isla can practice the mindfulness exercise on page 43
and visualize her safe place, welcoming her worry (about being
lost) into her house. By welcoming her worry into her house, she is
accepting that her worry is there. Once Isla accepts and befriends
her worry, she can focus on what to do next to find her aunt and
help herself feel better. She comes up with a plan to ask a store
manager to page her aunt. Her aunt comes to get her, and they go
home and enjoy their sleepover and ice cream.

CHAPTER SIX

Mysteriously Missing Homework

It's May, and Caleb hasn't missed a single homework assignment all year. Last year, he had a hard time keeping track of his assignments and getting things in on time, but not this year! His mom helped him set up a planner to keep track of his assignments. He has worked hard to keep it up to date and turn things in when they're due. He is proud of himself and his perfect homework record!

When Caleb's teacher starts to collect last night's spelling worksheet, he realizes that his homework isn't in his backpack. He starts to feel nervous. "That's weird," he thinks. He knows he did it. He remembers working on it last night at Dan's house while he waited for his mom to pick him up. He thought he had put it in his backpack, but where is it? Now Caleb is worried. What if he forgot his homework at Dan's house? He feels his body tense up, and he starts to sweat.

Caleb is frustrated. He thinks, "How could I let this happen? How could I have been so careless?" He thinks about how hard he has worked all year to turn in his assignments on time. Now here he is, almost done with the year, and he lost an assignment! Caleb is angry at himself. "How could I have done this?" He is worried that this is going to ruin his perfect homework record.

Caleb has trouble focusing the rest of class because he is worried about ruining his perfect homework record. This makes him even more frustrated, and he blames himself for not being able to focus. Because he is so distracted, he doesn't do well on an in-class assignment. Then he forgets to write down his next homework assignment. Later at lunch, his friends try to cheer him up, but he is too grumpy. His friends play a game together, but Caleb sits off to the side and misses out on the fun.

Everyone Has Feelings

Mindfulness is not about being perfect, and it's not about having the perfect reaction to everything that happens. Mindfulness is about accepting ourselves and remembering that we are doing the best we can in each moment. There will be days where you feel like you can handle anything, and there will be days where things may feel overwhelming. It can be hard not to feel disappointed in ourselves when we make mistakes. Remember our tricky brains—they like to notice the things that are going wrong. When we notice what we're doing wrong, it's easy to wish we had done things differently and then get mad with ourselves because we didn't.

Think about Caleb, who gets mad at himself for making a silly little mistake. He's worried about ruining his perfect homework record and mad at himself for being careless. He's judging himself and his mistake. But are his judgments helpful? Are they changing anything? No. His worry won't make his homework appear in his backpack—it's just making it harder for him to get through the rest of his day. He has trouble focusing in class and forgets to write down his next homework assignment. Even after his friends try to cheer him up, he misses out on the fun they have at lunch.

What do you think would have happened if Caleb had been kinder to himself and accepted his mistakes? When we notice that we are not being nice to ourselves, it's important to practice kindness. No one is always perfect, but we all still deserve love.

Mindfulness Exercise

Get into a comfortable position. You can either sit or lie down. If possible, keep your back straight so your breath can come easily. Close your eyes (or find something still to look at). Take a couple moments to focus on your breathing. Breathe in. Breathe out.

Repeat the following phrases either out loud or to yourself:

I am doing my best.

I am allowed to make mistakes.

I love myself.

I am doing my best.

I am allowed to make mistakes.

I love myself.

Rest easy knowing that you are doing your best, that you are allowed to make mistakes, and that you deserve love. And when you have doubts about yourself—because that is normal—repeat these phrases again and again.

It's Okay to Feel This Way

ACTIVITY: Time to help Caleb cheer up! Write down three nice things Caleb could say to himself—three things that are kind and accepting of his mistakes. I'll get you started with the first one:

I made a mistake and left my homework at Dan's house, and that is okay!

_____

_____

_____

_____

_____

_____

_____

ACTIVITY: **Now it's time to be your own cheerleader! Write down three nice things about yourself. The next time you hear yourself judging your actions, look back at these things and remind yourself how AWESOME you are!**

_____

_____

_____

_____

_____

_____

_____

Wrap Up

Let's go back to when Caleb is in class and notices that he is starting to feel worried and angry with himself. Maybe he notices a thought like, "How could I have been so careless?" Or maybe he notices that his body is tense. He can take a moment to close his eyes, take a couple of deep breaths, and repeat the mindfulness exercise on page 53. Taking the time to slow down and be kind to himself can help Caleb get through his uncomfortable feelings and be present for the rest of his day. He can participate in class and have fun with his friends. Then, when those thoughts of self-doubt return later (because remember, that is normal), he can say the three nice things about himself that he wrote down.

CHAPTER SEVEN

Keep Going!

Congratulations! You have learned important mindfulness skills and are ready to continue practicing mindfulness outside of this book.

It is helpful to practice these skills every day, so keep this book close so you can look at it when you need it. Remember, your brain is tricky. It can easily fall back into worried thinking. But now you know how to train your brain. You have the power to slow down and choose what thoughts you will listen to. You are in control.

Will practicing mindfulness be easy? Not at first. It's hard to train our brains to do something new, but you can do it! I like to think of it like this:

Imagine you are walking outside, and you come to a river that you need to cross. There are two bridges. One is big, wide, and sturdy, and there are many people going across it. This big, strong bridge represents our worried thoughts. You have been thinking these worried thoughts for a while now, and they have built a pretty strong bridge that your brain can easily use.

The other bridge is narrow and looks unstable. It swings back and forth when the wind blows, and no one else is on it. This bridge represents our new mindful thoughts and skills. You have only just learned them. They are new, so it will take practice. The more you practice, the stronger that bridge will become, and it will be easier and easier to get across it. Before you know it, that bridge will be the one that you brain always uses, and you will be practicing mindfulness without even realizing it!

Practice your mindful skills, and talk to your friends and family about them. Find a comfortable place to practice your mindfulness exercises. Build your mindful bridge! If you get stuck, reach out to a supportive adult for help.

Remember that you will have worries again, because worrying is part of your brain's job. What do you do the next time you are worried?

- **PAUSE:** Take a short break. You don't have to walk away to get a break, but if you can, that's great! If you can't walk away, just take a "mental break." Pause what you are doing, and take a deep breath.

- **NOTICE:** Pay attention to how your body feels. Is your body giving you warning signs that something is wrong? What are they? What thoughts are you having now? Are they helpful?

- **PRACTICE:** Use one of the mindfulness exercises in this book— choose the one that best works for you in the moment.

And remember, everyone makes mistakes. You do not have to be perfect to practice mindfulness. You can practice mindfulness whenever or wherever you are.

Mindfulness for Me

ACTIVITY: Draw a picture of yourself practicing mindfulness.

Draw your picture here:

How do you feel after drawing the picture? Do you feel calmer? Happier? You can take that feeling with you wherever you go.

ACTIVITY: Take a minute to find a mirror and repeat these words to yourself:

"I am here. I am present. I am in control."

Repeat these three sentences to yourself whenever you start to feel anxious. Let these words guide you and remind you of what you learned from this book. Our worries tend to take us away from the present moment. But you are here, you are present, and YOU are in control. Let these words remind you of the power you have within yourself to manage your worries.

CHAPTER EIGHT

For Parents, Teachers, and Counselors

In this section, parents and other supportive adults will find tips and guidelines for helping kids control their worries while using mindfulness. By getting this book for your child or the children you work with, you've already helped them take an important step on the road toward managing their anxiety.

Notes and Tips for Dealing with Anxious Behavior in Children

As you embark on this journey, set an intention for yourself and how you want to support your child. Do you want to give them more space and control? Do you want to be more supportive and present? Do you want to find a way to have more fun with them?

When interacting with anyone, including our children, it is easy to fall into patterns of communication that may not always be helpful (e.g., raising your voice, ignoring someone, using guilt to influence, etc.). Setting an intention guides our interactions with our children, helping us to remember what is most important. Set your intention here:

I will

Feel free to share your intention with your child!

No matter your intention, our focus should always be on being the best support we can be for our children. One of the most important ways to do this is to truly listen to them, with the goal of understanding them. Often as parents we go into conversations with our kids with the intention of solving their problems. When we do this, we are thinking about what we will say instead of what our children are actually saying to us. Let go of whatever you think you know, and go into the next conversation with your child with an open mind. This can be hard. As you begin to listen this way, it can help to repeat back to them (in your own words) what you think they are trying to say to make sure you understand.

You can also ask them how you can support them. Don't assume that you always know what is best for them. Let them guide you for what they need. Ask questions, and stay involved in their mindfulness practice.

Seeing our children in an anxious state can be difficult and upsetting. Be aware of your own reaction to your child's anxiety and how it affects them. Take time to observe how your child responds to what you say and do in response to their anxiety. Is there an area where you could do things a bit differently to be a more effective support? Remember that it's okay to be open about your own struggles with anxiety and what works for you, but this is about them. Their anxiety may look different from yours, as will their strategies for dealing with it.

Finally, familiarize yourself with the terms in the book. When you are both speaking the same language, it will be easier to ensure you're on the same page.

Mindful Practices for at Home and in the Classroom

Practice is important for building mindfulness skills. Here are some tips for how to build on the mindfulness skills discussed in this book and incorporate them into your everyday life.

First, start labeling emotions. Talk about your own, and make note of the ones you see in your child. Talk to them about why you think they are feeling a certain way. For instance, if you can tell your child is mad at you, tell them why you think that. "You aren't looking at me, and you haven't talked to me. Normally you are pretty chatty and look me in the eyes. Are you upset with me?" Increasing awareness of how we are feeling and how we show those feelings is an important first step when practicing mindfulness.

Next, work on understanding the thoughts that affect how they are feeling. Ask them what they are thinking when they are struggling. Listen, and validate their experiences. If they are too emotional in the moment, don't push it—talk to them about it later.

Even when your child isn't exhibiting worry, you can help them engage their senses and notice things that are going on around them. When you are out and about, just talk about what you see. "Oh, wow! Look at that big truck!" "Oh, what is that delicious smell?" Our senses are a powerful grounding tool that can be used to bring us back to the present moment. Helping our kids engage this skill when they are calm lays the foundation for using this skill when they are upset.

It's also important to give them time to slow down. This may mean saying no to some weekend events or signing up for fewer activities. But all kids, especially kids who struggle with worries and anxiety, need time and space to decompress and process everything that is going on in their world.

To facilitate this, help them create a space where they can practice their mindfulness skills. It should be a place that is just for them, with some objects that they find comforting and comfortable. It doesn't have to be a huge space. Sometimes even just a special pillow is enough. The idea is that we want them to have a place where they have some control. They can go to this space and choose how to help themselves in the moment. This should not be somewhere you force them to go, but rather a space you can offer.

Above all, talk to them about what they are learning in this book—and learn the material with them. Use the language that this book uses throughout the day. Help them familiarize themselves with the topics and practices. While children can use this book on their own, adult guidance can be essential in ensuring they get the most out of the activities and apply them to their everyday lives.

Guidelines for Going through These Exercises with Children

- Make sure to ask them if they want you to do the activities with them or if they would like you to take a step back. Respect their wishes while trying to stay involved.

- Follow their lead! Let them decide the ways they're comfortable interacting with and using the book.

- Talk to them about the concepts discussed in the book, using the same language. Consistency and repetition are important.

- Give them enough time and space to use the book to their best ability.

Acknowledgments

To my children: Carter, Ellie Gray, Rowan, and Koa. Becoming a parent has been one of the most complex and overwhelming journeys of my life. Thank you for being my guides on what has become a spiritual adventure. You have reminded me of the magic that is waiting for us in each moment, and I am forever humbled and honored to be your mom.

To my husband, Joe. Thank you for your unwavering support of my passions and mindfulness journey. You believed in me before I believed in myself, and I am eternally grateful to be your partner on this crazy adventure.

To my tribe of friends and family who support me. This book could not have happened without each and every one of you. I have been blessed with such a wonderful village.

And to my parents, Terry and Maureen Hurley, whose foundation of unconditional love made all of this possible. Being your daughter is one of the truest honors of my life.